MEL BAY PRESENTS
TECHNICAL DEVELO[PMENT]
FOR THE CLARINE[TIST]
SCALES, CHORDS, ETUDES AND PRACTICE ROUTINES

MB97190

BY NORMAN M. HEIM

BILL'S MUSIC SHELF

Introduction

This book consists of scales, chords and routines which are written for the technical advancement of the intermediate level clarinetist. The material is presented with varied articulations, meters, rhythms, and dynamics in order to enhance the experience of the clarinetist.

The emphasis for most of the book is placed on materials in keys through four accidentals, using the major and minor scheme. More advanced keys and scale patterns are presented later in the book along with routines which may be used as daily warmup material.

For keys through four accidentals the following order of material is used in order to be consistent and complete:

a. Major scale
b. Major chord
c. Minor scale
d. Minor chord
e. Augmented chord
f. Diminished chord
g. Major scale in thirds
h. Minor scale in thirds
i. Chromatic scale
j. Major scale in fourths
k. Major scale in fifths
l. Major scale in Octaves
m. Returning scale routine
n. Mechanism study
o. Etude

Each of the scales, chords and routines have suggested dynamic markings and breaths in order to make each item a musical experience. All technical material should be played musically. However, the purpose of having technical studies is to develop technical speed with control. Therefore, many scales, chords and routines can be accomplished with one breath when the technique has been mastered.

Each item is written with a specified articulations. However, the player can use different articulations in order to develop all aspects of technical development. All suggested markings in the book can be modified in order to fit the needs of the player.

Although each key is presented with a methodical and concise plan, the material need not be studied in the order of presentation, but should fit the specific needs of the performer. Certain exercises can be skipped and picked up later in the development of the player.

The stylistic content of the music in this book reflects the musical styles prevalent in the eighteenth and nineteenth centuries. The scales and chord patterns found in the twentieth century require separate study. The mastering of the materials in this book will give a clarinetist good technical facility to play music written before the twentieth century, and will give a good technical background for playing contemporary music.

March, 1993
Norman M. Heim
Hyattsville, Maryland

Table of Contents

Glossary for Alternate Fingering Symbols

1. S - indicates use of the appropriate side Key(s).

2. r - indicates use of key with small finger (fifth) of right hand.

3. L - indicates use of key with small finger (fifth) of left hand.

4. $\frac{1}{1}$ - symbol for   alternate fingering for E-flat (D-sharp) or clarion register note B-flat (A-sharp)

5. $\frac{1}{2}$ - symbol for   alternate fingering for E-flat (D-sharp)

   or clarion register note B-flat (A-sharp)

6. × - indicates chromatic fingering to be used

Keys of C Major and A Minor

a. C Major Scale

b. C Major Chord

c. A Minor Scale

d. A Minor Chord

e. C Augmented Chord

f. Diminished Chord (key of C)

g. C Minor Scale in Thirds

h. A Minor Scale in Thirds

i. Chromatic Scale on C

j. C Major Scale in Fourths

2

k. C Major Scale in Fifths

l. C Major Scale in Octaves

m. C Major Returning Scale

n. C Major Mechanism Study

o. Etude in C Major

Keys of F Major and D Minor

a. F Major Scale

b. F Major Chord

c. D Minor Scale

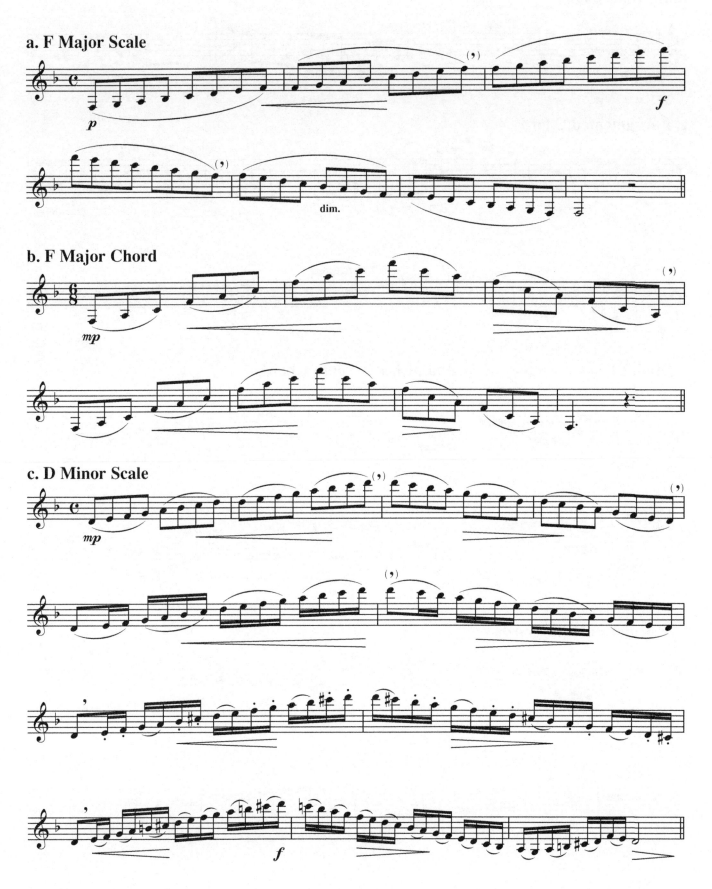

d. D Minor Chord

e. F Augmented Chord

f. Diminished Chord (key of F), diminished Seventh Chord

g. F Major Scale in Thirds

h. D Minor Scale in Thirds

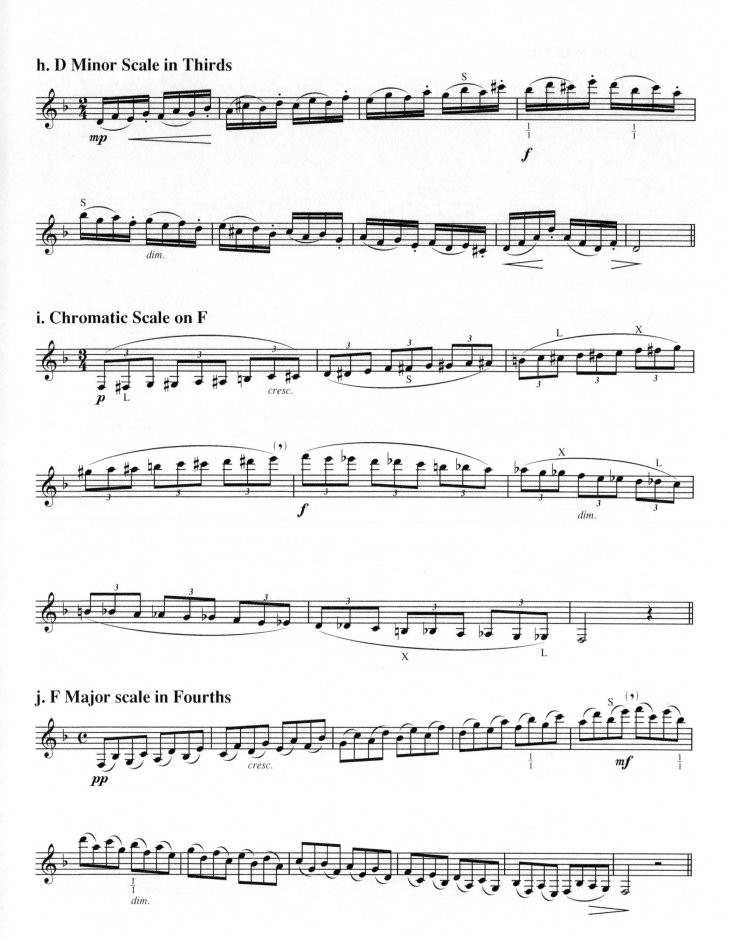

i. Chromatic Scale on F

j. F Major scale in Fourths

k. F Major Scale in Fifths

l. F Major Scale in Octaves

m. F Major Returning Scale

n. F Major Mechanism Study

o. Etude in F Major

9

Keys of G Major and E Minor

a. G Major Scale

b. G Major Chord

c. E Minor Scale

11

d. E Minor Chord

e. G Augmented Chord

f. Diminished Chord (key of G) and Diminished seventh Chord

g. G Major Scale in Thirds

h. E Minor Scale in Thirds

i. Chromatic Scale on G

j. G Major Scale in Fourths

k. G Major Scale in Fifths

l. G Major in Octaves

m. G Major Returning Scale

n. G Major Mechanism Study

14

o. Etude in G Major

16

Keys of B-Flat Major and G Minor

a. B-Flat Major Scale

b. B-flat Major Chord

c. G Minor Scale

d. G Minor Chord

e. B-Flat Augmented Chord

f. Diminished Chord (Key of B-Flat Major) and Diminished Seventh Chord

g. B-Flat Major Scale in Thirds

h. G Minor Scale in Thirds

i. Chromatic Scale on B Flat

j. B-Flat Major Scale in Fourths

k. B-Flat Major Scale in Fifths

l. B-Flat Major Scale in Octaves

m. B-Flat Major Returning Scale

19

n. B-Flat Major Mechanism Study

o. Etude in B-Flat Major

21

Keys of D Major and B Minor

a. D Major Scale

b. D Major Chord

c. B Minor Scale

d. B Minor Chord

e. D Augmented Chord

f. Diminished Chord (Key of D Major) and diminished seventh chord

g. D Major Scale in Thirds

h. B Minor Scale in Thirds

i. Chromatic Scale on D

23

j. D Major Scale in Fourths

k. D Major Scale in Fifths

l. D Major Scale in Octaves

m. D Major Returning Scale

n. D Major Mechanism

o. Etude in D Major

Keys of E-Flat Major and C Minor

a. E-flat Major Scale

b. E-Flat Major Chord

c. C Minor Scale

d. C Minor Chord

27

e. E-flat Augmented Chord

f. Diminished Chord (key of E-Flat Major) and Diminished Seventh Chord

g. E-flat Major Scale in Thirds

h. C Minor Scale in Thirds

i. Chromatic Scale on E-Flat

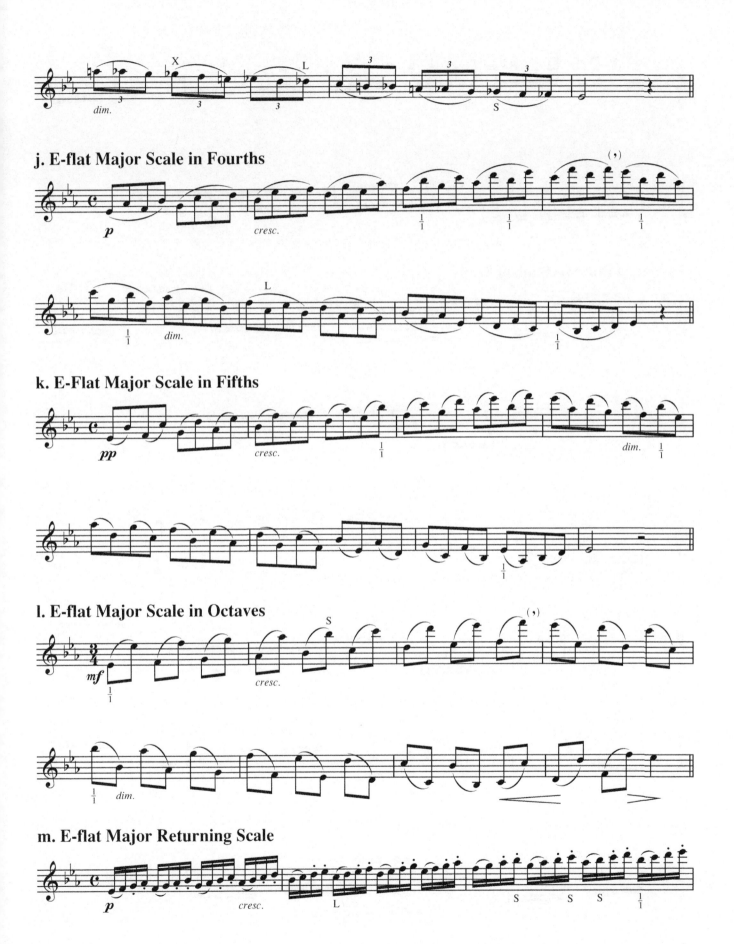

j. E-flat Major Scale in Fourths

k. E-Flat Major Scale in Fifths

l. E-flat Major Scale in Octaves

m. E-flat Major Returning Scale

n. E-flat Major Mechanism Study

o. Etude in E-flat Major

Keys of A Major and F-Sharp Minor

a. A Major Scale

b. A Major Chord

c. F-sharp Minor Scale

d. F-sharp Minor Chord

e. A Augmented Chord

f. Diminished Chord (key of A Major) and Diminished Seventh Chord

g. A Major Scale in Thirds

h. F-sharp Minor Scale in Thirds

i. Chromatic Scale on A

33

j. A Major Scale in Fourths

k. A Major Scale in Fifths

l. A Major Scale in Octaves

m. A Major Returning Scale

n. A Major Mechanism Study

o. Etude in A Major

36

Keys of A-Flat Major and F Minor

a. A-flat Major Scale

b. A-flat Major Chord

c. F Minor Scale

d. F Minor Chord

e. A-Flat Augmented Chord

f. Diminished Chord (Key of A-flat Major) and Diminished Seventh chord

g. A-flat Major Scale in Thirds

h. F Minor Scale in Thirds

i. Chromatic Scale on A-flat

j. A-flat Major Scale in Fourths

k. A-flat Major Scale in Fifths

l. A-flat Major Scale in Octaves

m. A-flat Major Returning Scale

40

n. A-flat Major Mechanism Study

o. Etude in A-flat Major

41

42

Keys of E Major and C-sharp Minor

a. E Major Scale

b. E Major Chord

c. C-sharp Minor Scale

d. C-sharp Minor Chord

e. E Augmented Chord

f. Diminished Chord (Key of E Minor) and Diminished Seventh Chord

g. E Major Scale in Thirds

h. C-sharp Minor Scale in Thirds

i. Chromatic Scale on E

j. E Major Scale in Fourths

k. E Major Scale in Fifths

45

l. E Major Scale in Octaves

m. E Major Returning Scale

n. E Major Mechanism Study

o. Etude in Major

47

48

Major Scale and Chords with Five, Six and Seven Accidentals

a. D-flat Major Scale

b. D-flat Major Chord

c. B-Major Scale

49

d. B Major Chord

e. G-flat Major Scale

f. G-flat Major Chord

g. F-sharp Major (same sound as G-flat Major)

h. F-sharp Major Chord

i. C-flat Major Scale (same sound as B Major)

j. C-flat Major Chord

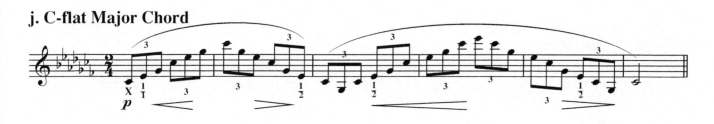

k. C-sharp Major Scale (same sound as D-flat Major)

l. C-sharp Major Scale Chord

Minor Scales and Chords with Five, Six and Seven Accidentals

a. B-flat Minor Scale

b. B-flat Minor Chord

c. G-sharp Minor Scale

d. G-sharp Minor Chord

e. E-flat Minor Chord

f. E-flat Minor Chord

g. D-sharp Minor Scale (same sound as E-flat Minor Scale)

h. D-sharp Minor Chord

i. A-flat Minor Scale

j. A-flat Minor Chord

k. A-sharp Minor Scale (same sound as B-flat Minor)

l. A-sharp Minor Chord

Other Scales

The following scales can be transferred (transposed) to all keys. Each Scale is presented here in two keys.

a. Hungarian Minor Scale on A

b. Hungarian Minor Scale on C

c. Gapped Scale on C

d. Gapped Scale on G

e. Dorian Scale on D

f. Dorian Scale on E

g. Mixolydian Scale on G

h. Mixolydian Scale on F

i. Aeolian Scale on A

j. Aelian Scale on D

Dominant Seventh Chords

a. Dominant Seventh Chord on G

b. Dominant Seventh Chord on C

c. Dominant Seventh Chord on D

d. Dominant Seventh Chord on F

e. Dominant Seventh Chord on A

f. Dominant Seventh Chord on B-flat

g. Dominant Seventh Chord on E

h. Dominant Seventh Chord on E-flat

i. Dominant Seventh on B

Daily Routines

a. Major Scale Routine

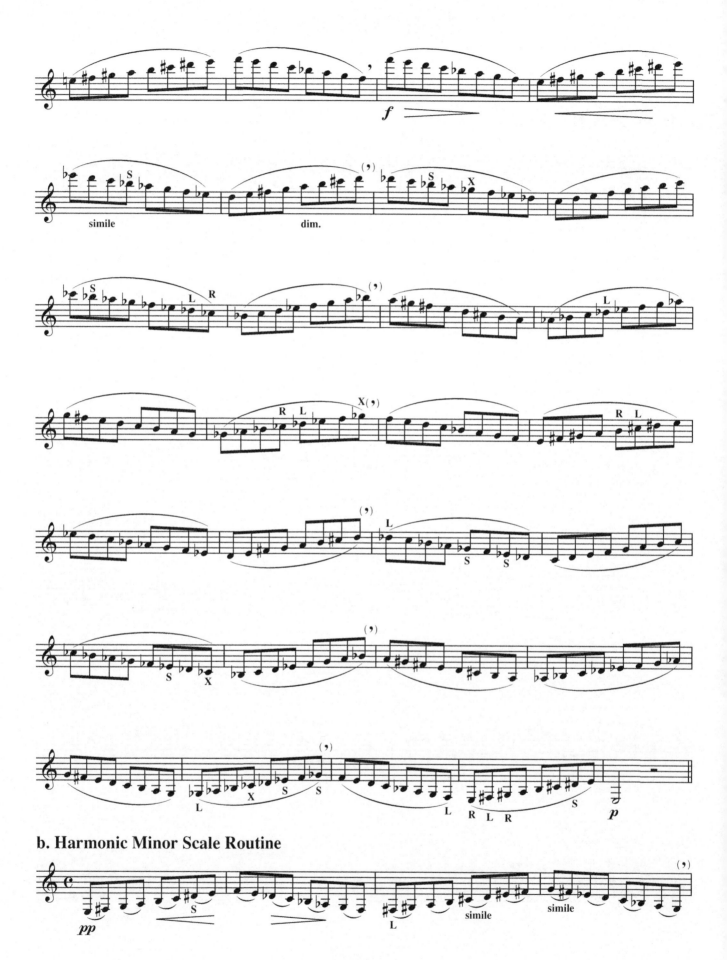

b. Harmonic Minor Scale Routine

61

c. Major Chord Routine

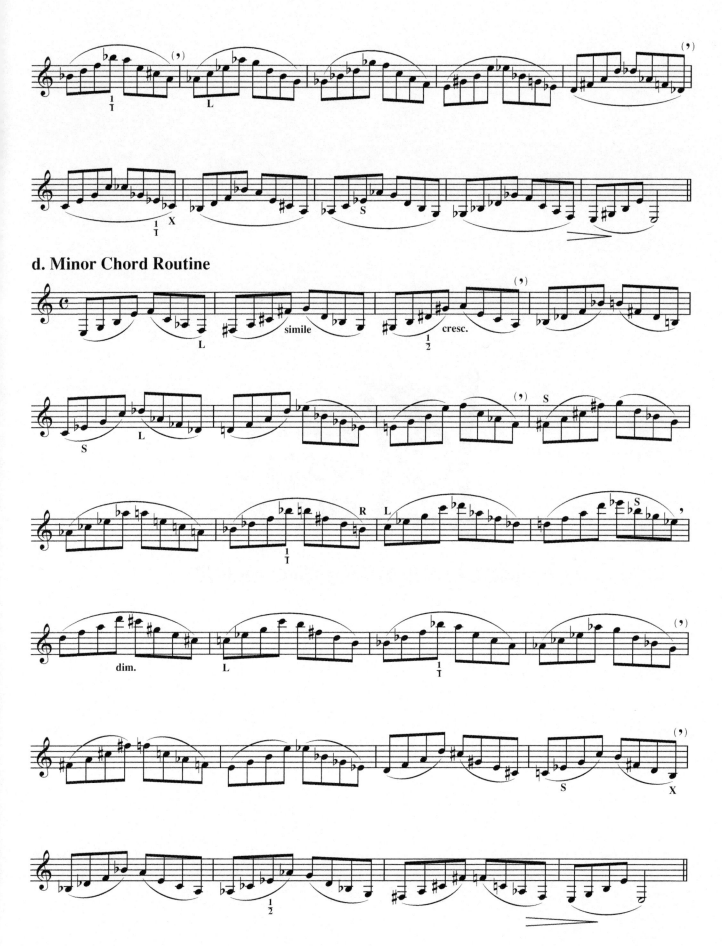

d. Minor Chord Routine

UNIQUELY INTERESTING MUSIC!

Printed in Great Britain
by Amazon

33748987R00040